MAXIMIZE YOUR ~~DISABILITIES~~

Living with CAPD

Text © & Illustration © 2012 by Christopher Rawlins
Designed by Christopher Rawlins

ISBN 13: 978-1494991920
ISBN 10: 1494991926

Published by Christopher Rawlins
Printed by CreateSpace 2014

Written and Illustrated by Christopher Rawlins

● crawlinsgraphics.com ●

I dedicate this book to my parents and to my brother Jesse. Their continued love and support motivated me to create this book. I appreciate all you have done for me and love you all very much.

I also dedicate this book to ALL children, especially children with APD/CAPD or any other kind of disability. I hope this will give them encouragement and confidence in themselves so they can succeed in whatever they wish to accomplish in life.

I want to thank everyone from my Thesis class for their advice and support. A special thanks to my family and my extended family for the time they spent guiding me through the self publishing process. Thank you for believing in me!

-Chris Rawlins

Many years ago, a healthy baby boy was born. Although this boy was born without any problems, he struggled with learning how to read, speak and listen the same way as other boys and girls his age. His difficulties with language made him stand out. He was different from other children at school.

The boy was often left alone in class. On the playground his classmates would leave him behind. The little boy tried his best to play with the other kids, but they would only laugh and make fun of him. They made him feel sad and unwanted. He was scared that he would never fit in with the rest of the kids.

The young boy's name was Max. He was a smart child, and although he wanted to learn, he had a hard time understanding new words and talking with others. Some of the easiest words for most kids his age were too hard for Max. Max soon came to realize that he had challenges that other kids his age did not have. These challenges came from a condition called CAPD (Central Auditory Processing Disorder).

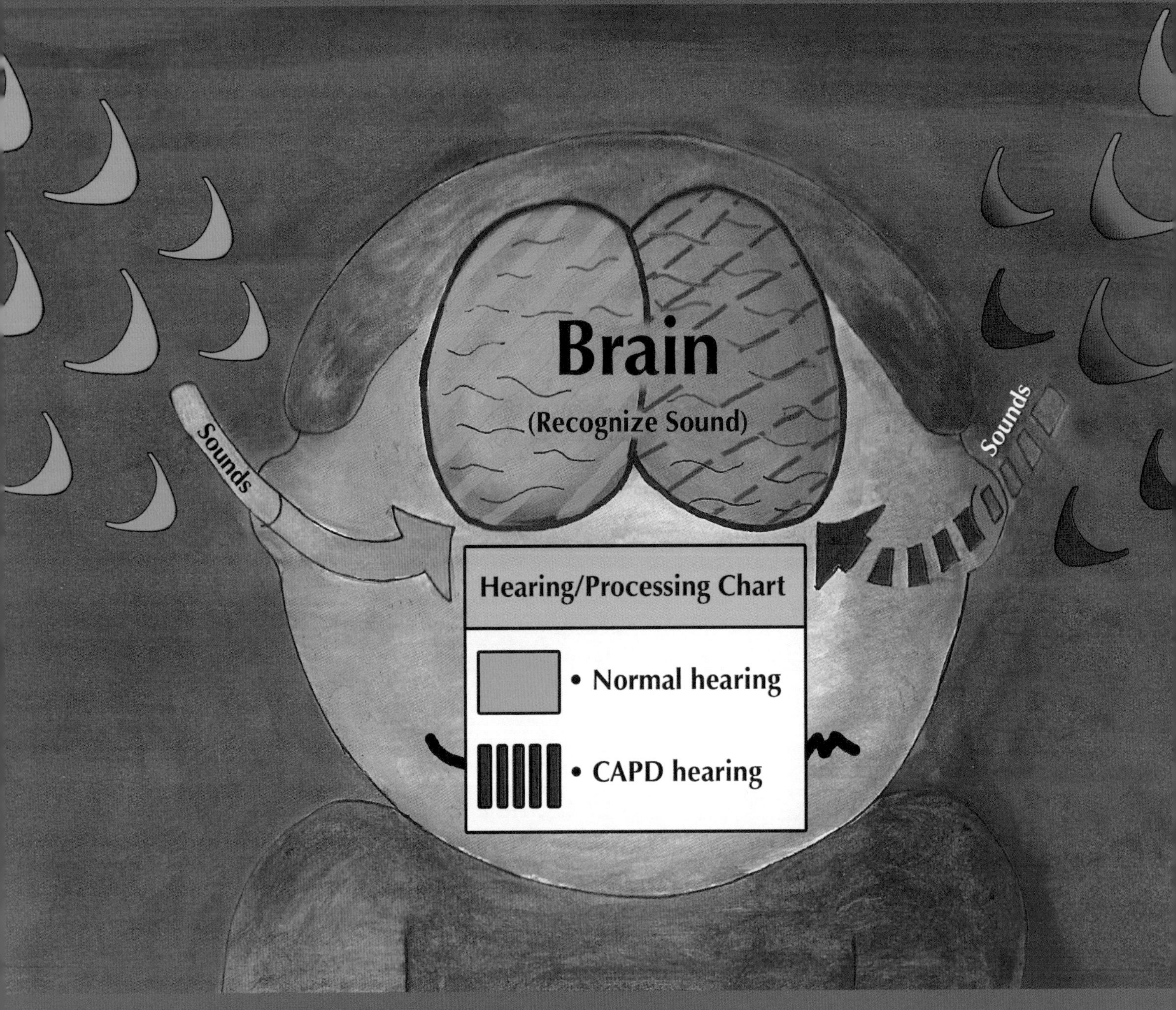
Brain
(Recognize Sound)
Sounds
Sounds
Hearing/Processing Chart
• Normal hearing
• CAPD hearing

CAPD is a disorder that affects both kids and adults. People with CAPD cannot process information normally because their ears and brains do not match up completely. CAPD is not a hearing disability that has to do with volume or hearing loss. Instead, CAPD jumbles the way sounds are received by the processing center of the brain.

CAPD can vary from very mild to severe and affects each person differently. When people with CAPD hear someone talking, it takes longer for them to understand certain parts of the conversation, and this can delay their complete understanding of the message. The brain's messages are somewhat confused and this can cause problems, especially in school.

CAPD is similar to listening to a radio with very bad static or someone talking underwater. The sound is there but the words are unclear. As the background noise increases, it can become more difficult to understand what was said. As a result, people with CAPD often have difficulty with speech, language, making friends and keeping up with schoolwork.

Max learned how to speak much later than most other children. At first, Max could only make sounds and repeat certain words. When speaking, he usually pronounced words wrong and stuttered while trying to complete his thoughts.

Max also had a hard time looking directly in the eyes of others. Max would easily get frustrated when trying to have a conversation. He was unhappy that he could not focus during conversations and felt embarrassed when he could not get others to understand him.

Max's parents enrolled him in preschool early to help him improve his CAPD. Max also went to speech therapy several times per week. Max did improve a bit, but not by much. When Max later went to a higher grade, he had trouble learning and understanding what the teacher was saying. Learning was even more difficult if the teacher spoke too quickly or if it was too noisy in the classroom.

The later years in middle school were the most difficult for Max. The students called him names, treated him harshly, teased him and left him out. Max was smart and fun to be with but no one realized that.

Max had a very hard time fitting in with other children his age. Other kids often spoke too quickly and Max couldn't process the words fast enough. As time passed, his struggles stayed the same and Max began to avoid other kids all together in order to save himself from further embarrassment and frustration.

When Max began to speak, he sometimes stuttered and struggled to say what he truly wanted to say. When Max was finished talking, he usually felt awkward, especially if the listener stared at him with a look of confusion. Max wished he could speak as easily as the other kids.

What hurt Max the most was being teased and bullied by his classmates. This made Max more nervous as he tried to stand up to the other children. The more nervous Max became, the more difficult it was to defend himself.

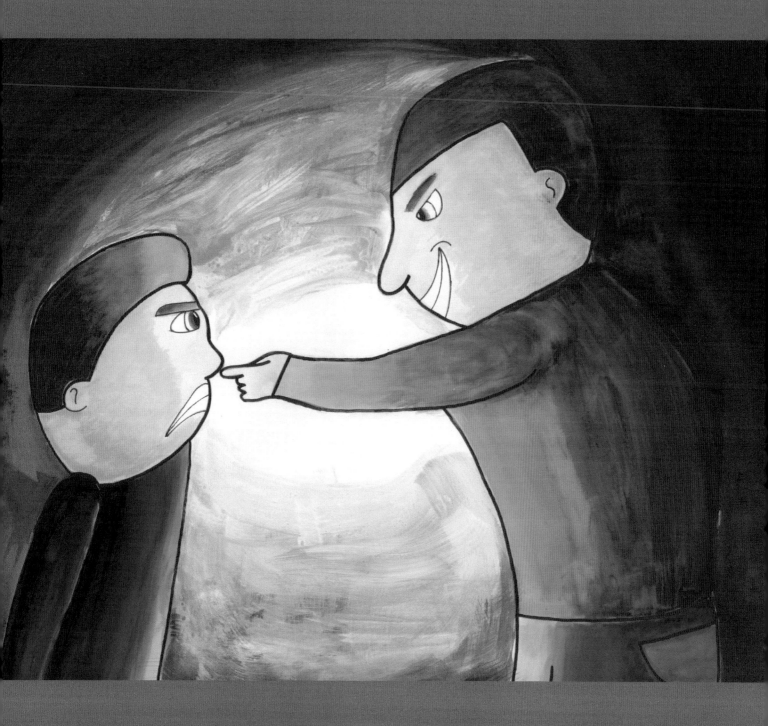

Every time Max came home from school, he felt sad and lonely. His level of confidence decreased. Sometimes he felt that he would rather stay at home than deal with more pain at school. Max felt best in the safety and comfort of his home. His only two comforts were his family and drawing.

To keep Max's spirits up, his parents gave him coloring books and crayons because he really enjoyed coloring and drawing. Max soon moved on from coloring books and started to draw pictures based on his own imagination. His first character had the super powers that Max wished he had himself. His name was Super Max and he had his very own comic book series.

Max also used pencils, markers, paint and pastels to expand his art skills. He soon realized that drawing helped him escape from his problems. Even if only for a little while, Max felt that all of his troubles disappeared when he was drawing.

Max had great visual skills and this helped develop his artistic talents. Due to his disability, Max had to be very organized. Because of this, he was often the most prepared student in his classes. Most importantly, Max was a very smart person and didn't like being judged unfairly because of his CAPD.

Having CAPD does not mean one's mind is flawed, it is just wired differently. Most of the time, Max was able to learn easily just by watching other people. Max learned visually and was fueled by his own curiosity and strong will to succeed. Max's motto was to never give up!

With much support and help from his family, Max's learning skills improved. He found ways to make studying easier for himself, including working in a quiet environment, using handouts, enrolling in smaller classes, reading things repeatedly, and building his vocabulary. After many years of speech therapy and hard work, Max gained the confidence he needed to fit in with others and he slowly began to make friends. This made Max happy and gave him strength to keep moving forward.

None of this would have been possible without determination and a positive attitude. Although Max struggled with language and processing, he never gave up and worked through his challenges to succeed. Max worked hard in school, eventually earned an art degree in college and became a graphic design artist. Max is very proud of his accomplishments and is very grateful for all of the people who helped and supported him along the way. Although living with CAPD was challenging for Max, he learned to focus on his abilities rather than his disability. Once he knew how to maximize his potential, he could succeed in whatever life had to offer.

If you want to learn more about Central Auditory Processing Disorder (CAPD) especially if you think your child may have these symptoms; check out the following resources for more information and important strategies for you and your child.

Websites

• http://kidshealth.org

• http://www.asha.org

• http://www.ncld.org

Books/Articles

• *Learning Disabilities Sourcebook (Health Reference Series: Vol: 33)* by Linda M. Shin

• *Understanding Auditory Processing Disorders in Children* by Teri James Bellis

• *When the Brain Can't Hear: Unraveling the Mystery of Auditory Processing Disorder* by Teri James Bellis

Medical Centers in the US

• Children's Specialized Hospital, Mountainside, NJ - *Early Intervention, Audiology, CAPD Testing, Speech Therapy*

• Hackensack University Medical Center, Hackensack, NJ - *Audiology, CAPD Testing, Cochlear Implant program, Rehab Services*

• Somerset Medical Center, Somervile, NJ - *Speech, Voice and Swallowing Center*

- St. Joseph's Children's Hospital, Patterson, NJ - *Child Development Center - Developmental and Behavioral Pediatrics*

- Northeast Health: St Peter's Health Partners, Troy, NY - *Hearing Center*

- Stony Brook University Hospital, Stony Brook, NY - *Hearing Services*

- University of Rochester Medical Center, Rochester, NY - *Audiology*

- Memorial Medical Center, Springfield, Illinois - *Hearing Center*

- Vanderbilt University Medical Center, Nashvile, TN - *Hearing and Speech*

- Cincinnati Children's Hospital Medical Center, Cincinnati, Ohio - *Language / Auditory Processing Disorder*

- The California Ear Institute, Palo Alto, CA - *Hearing Device Center*

- Fisher-Titus Medical Center, Norwalk, OH - *Rehabilitation Center - Speech-Language Pathology, Audiology*

Never give up!

Thanks for reading!

If you want to contact the author, please visit this site:

crawlinsgraphics.com

Made in the USA
Lexington, KY
15 May 2017